Heartfelt Poetry

Tania S. Valdés S.

BookLeaf
Publishing

Presentation by *BookLeaf Publishing*

Web: www.bookleafpub.com

E-mail: info@bookleafpub.com

ISBN: 9789357615617

First edition 2023

Dedicated to my loved ones, especially to the strongest individuals I know, my daughters, Tavania and Mireya.

With Love in His Eyes

He looked at her with love in his eyes
She wasn't certain if to love him back
He drew her close
She pushed away
Mixed feelings; frozen
She was too scared to love again
And as she walked away
He looked at her with love in his eyes

Abuse

Strong and tough
Cold-hearted at times
cause no one knows the feelings inside
Happy home
Happy life
Yet, what happens behind closed doors
remains in the dark
Don't dare to say, you might be judged
Abuse
Can happen to anyone

Alone

Feeling blue
Alone and with reasons unknown

Depression
The phone rings and messages beep
Yet, you still feel alone
Sitting in the dark with uncontrollable thoughts
Reaching out is an option
But you don't know how
Who's hand to hold.
Need a shoulder to lean on
Someone to listen
Someone who cares
But who would love me enough?
So, I'm back in the room, alone
Depression
The silent killer

Affection

The beat of your heart
takes my breath away
Feeling you close, it's like heaven itself
Hold me in your arms
where I can feel safe
Don't ever leave me
My love
My best friend

Free

5

Broken heart and into pieces
I'm torn apart and I try not to cry

These wounds
These scars
Feeling trapped in this pain
that consumes me day and night
But I'll find a way
A way
to set myself free

Courage

Courage
When you fight your own battles
and hold back the tears
When you deal with mental health
and the fear of the unknown
Courage
It's finding any strength that's hidden within
To stand alone even though you're afraid
because in one's mind
It's all you know

Goodbye

The sudden parting of ways
You never said goodbye
It broke my heart to lose you
but I understand "Why"
When God called you home
was to relieve you from your pain,
and even though I miss you dearly
in my heart you hold a place

The Older You Get

The older you get
the smarter you should become
when choosing the people;
You want in your life
It's not what they offer, give or buy
It's the loyalty of friendship, love and time
So as you get older;
Know what you want
because the abundance of quality is a priority in
life

Have You Ever

Have you ever felt sad with your chest so tight
holding back the tears, all choked up?
Have you ever felt overwhelmed
where you just wanna run
to escape the pain consuming you inside?
Have you ever felt so alone
Surrounded by a crowd?

Have you ever?

Hungry for Love

His hands so strong yet soft
Pulls me close
Grabs me tight
Our heartbeats now beat as one
He kisses me slowly yet passionate and deep
I close my eyes as I am lost in his kiss
because I too; am hungry for love

Seasons

11

Hot sunny days
the beach cools you down
relaxing under a garden shade
BBQ times with family gathered around
Cooler and darker days
Colourful leaves on the ground
Goodbye warmer seasons
Hello colder ones

Untitled

Lost soul
Unwanted
Unloved
You reach out
But no one is there

Don't Ever

Don't be a fool
Don't be afraid
 Never settle for any less
Always have the courage
the courage to never change
Change those commas to a final end

Beauty

Beauty; it's not just what you see;
the physical or a pretty face
Beauty also comes within
From the heart, mind and soul
It's a combination of beautiful qualities
Beauty is the fundamental purpose of humanity

Untitled

15

I didn't change
It is still me
The friend
The lover. The person you met
I didn't change
My dignity just kicked in
which taught me self-worth
And self-love hidden within

Untitled

16

She's strong
Takes care of herself
She ain't weak
She's Brave and Independent
She's tough
But most of the time,
The strongest ones are those who need love the
most

I Feel Like

17

I feel like screaming
Explode and cry
Devastated
Alone and in despair

No one to tell me; all is well
And as you look away,
I feel like giving up
I just want someone to hold me
until I can breathe again

My Love

What is your name?
What a beautiful sound
but I prefer the sound of
"My Love" coming out of my mouth.

Healed Myself

19

Patched my own wounds
Wiped my own tears
Picked up the pieces
and gave myself time to heal
Bit by bit
I put myself back together
Healed myself because I deserve better

The Eyes

If only you could see
behind the light in her eyes
All the fear and anxiety
she daily needs to fight
If only you could see
behind those beautiful eyes
The pain and struggles
she always carries inside
If only you could see
Perhaps you'll understand
that the window to someone's soul
is not always through the eyes

Focus On You

Focus on yourself
and everything you do
Don't worry about others
and what they say about you
Focus on your happiness, your love and peace of
mind
Love everything about you
even your flaws
So stop worrying
what others might think
Because the biggest commitment
should be fulfilling your needs
Start from scratch
If need to do;
Focus on you for a change
And just simply be you

<u>About the Author:</u> Born in South America, Chile, Tania currently lives in Toronto, Canada. She is a single mother of two beautiful, intelligent and independent daughters. The vivacious writer enjoys reading, poetry, puzzles, music, and a hot cup of coffee.

www.ingramcontent.com/pod-product-compliance
Lightning Source LLC
Chambersburg PA
CBHW070734160726
48003CB00006BA/2509